DEPRESSION

Proven Ways They Don't Want You to Know to Naturally Cure Depression for the Rest of Your Life

SARAH JONES

© Copyright 2017 by Sarah Jones. All Rights Reserved

This document is geared towards providing exact and reliable information in regards to the topic and issue covered. The publication is sold with the idea that the publisher is not required to render accounting, officially permitted, or otherwise, qualified services. If advice is necessary, legal or professional, a practiced individual in the profession should be ordered.

From a Declaration of Principles which was accepted and approved equally by a Committee of the American Bar Association and a Committee of Publishers and Associations.

In no way is it legal to reproduce, duplicate, or transmit any part of this document in either electronic means or in printed format. Recording of this publication is strictly prohibited and any storage of this document is not allowed unless with written permission from the publisher. All rights reserved.

The information provided herein is stated to be truthful and consistent, in that any liability, in terms of inattention or otherwise, by any usage or abuse of any policies, processes, or directions contained within is the solitary and utter responsibility of the recipient reader. Under no circumstances will any legal responsibility or blame be held against the publisher for any reparation, damages, or monetary loss due to the information herein, either directly or indirectly.

Respective authors own all copyrights not held by the publisher.

The information herein is offered for informational purposes solely, and is universal as so. The presentation of the information is without contract or any type of guarantee assurance.

The trademarks that are used are without any consent, and the publication of the trademark is without permission or backing by the trademark owner. All trademarks and brands within this book are for clarifying purposes only and are the owned by the owners themselves, not affiliated with this document.

Table of Contents

INTRODUCTION 1

Chapter 1: Depression: A General Overview 4

Chapter 2: 10 Effective Ways to Care for Yourself and Overcome Depression 8

Chapter 3: Natural Therapies for Depression 24

Chapter 4: 6 Ways to Fun Away Depression 34

Chapter 5: 4 Rituals to Inspire Happiness in Times of Depression 41

Chapter 6: Overcoming Depression While Dealing with a Thyroid Condition 49

Chapter 7: Dealing with Stress and Depression 59

Chapter 8: Dr. Ilardi's Therapeutic Lifestyle Change for Depression 67

Chapter 9: One Day at a Time: The 24-Hour Guide to Survive Depression 74

Chapter 10: Inspirational People and How They Overcame Depression 84

CONCLUSION 92

MORE BOOKS BY SARAH 93

INTRODUCTION

Depression is a common mental condition that affects many people. Caused by a combination of psychological, genetic, environmental, and biological factors, depression often prevents people from function normally in their daily lives and impedes their cognitive and physical abilities. The economic downward spiral experienced in almost every part of the world with the loss of jobs, poverty, hardships, heartbreaks, broken homes, and poor health has increased the global prevalence of this condition. Sadly, depression is often regarded as a myth, with typically sarcastic remarks saying that depressed people are overdoing it or dramatizing everything just to gain attention. This stigma leads people with depression to refuse treatment for fear of being discriminated against. This fear often triggers further downward spiraling, a fact that is often overlooked but is in dire need of attention from mental health practitioners.

Today, it is common to hear of people committing suicide almost every day simply because of their perceived inability to endure certain ugly situations. Apart from these external causes of depression, some biological factors can contribute to a depressive state, including hormonal imbalances that can further worsen a person's mental condition.

What is more frustrating is that it is more challenging to deal with depressive conditions caused by biological factors, because people who suffer from such cases often fail to realize the condition links to a biological cause and thus concentrate on external factors while ignoring the root cause of the problem. Most people find it easy to address the symptoms displayed at the surface, rather than tire themselves out by probing deeper to find the real cause. When depression is not tackled from the root cause, however, it worsens.

While a number of medical treatments for depression exist, they do not always deliver long-term results. Furthermore, most depressed individuals who use medication to manage the condition often relapse, since medication only suppresses the symptoms and is not ideal for long-term recovery.

As such, the best long-term strategy to overcome depression is through natural treatment methods that offer a way of resolving the source of the depression. This book offers various natural ways to kick out the depression menace and stay depression-free for the rest of your life.

In addition to these tips, this book shares the life lessons of Dr. Stephen Ilardi, Tony Robbins, and Douglas Bloch — seasoned life coaches and inspirational icons for people who are going through depression. Hopefully, these lessons will help inspire you and

DEPRESSION

wake up your inner strength to help you get on the road towards recovery.

Thanks again for purchasing this book. I hope you'll find within its pages the strength and hope to overcome your darkest days!

CHAPTER 1

Depression: A General Overview

Before we discuss these well-kept secrets, let's understand depression. Depression is a severe mood disorder that affects your feelings and thought patterns. It changes how you handle daily tasks, how well you sleep, and how you relate with the people in your life. It can negatively impact your eating habits, your job, your health, and your overall wellbeing.

Depression comes in different forms and is accompanied by a number of signs that could be psychological or physical. However, according to experts, to be diagnosed with major depression, these symptoms must be experienced for at least two consecutive weeks. Below are common symptoms of depression:

- Having trouble focusing, remembering things or making decisions.

- Self-loathing.

- Lack of energy.

- Irritability.

- Sleeping too much or not having adequate sleep.

- Loss of interest in your day-to-day activities.

- Having feelings of hopelessness and helplessness.

- Significant weight gain or weight loss.

- Engaging in reckless behavior like substance abuse, reckless driving or compulsive gambling.

According to the United States National Institute of Mental Health, it is common to see depression alongside other mental conditions such as obsessive-compulsive disorder, phobias, panic disorders, anxiety, and eating disorders.

Depression in children

Depression is not a common condition in children. As children grow, they are bound to experience different emotions and mood swings; however, these do not necessarily indicate that they are depressed. Experts consider a child depressed only when the child shows signs of sadness for several weeks in a row, in which case, you should seek professional help.

Another indication of possible depression in a child could be recurrent disruptive behaviors that interfere with the child's normal daily life, interest in school, social activities, family life, etc. According to the American National Institute of Mental Health, 1 out of every 33 children experiences depression.

Depression in adolescents

Among teens and adolescents, feeling unhappy is a common thing. However, whenever you observe signs of unhappiness in a teen that last for more than two weeks, along with other signs of depression, then the teen might be going through a case of adolescent depression. According to the American National Institute of Mental Health, 1 in every 8 adolescents experiences depression.

Depression in adults

Depression is a prevalent adult mental condition. Among adults, most cases of suicide and suicide attempts all over the world are depression instigated. In the United States alone, more than 15 million adults experience major depression during their lifetime. According to the United States National Institute of Mental Health, when compared to all other psychiatric conditions, depression poses the highest suicide risk among adults.

Depression and the brain

According to a report published by psycheducation.org, depression affects parts of the brain such as the hippocampus—the part of the limbic system that regulates emotions and memory formation—by reducing its size. The shrinkage of the hippocampus comes from the excessive release of the hormone called cortisol. Cortisol inhibits the uptake of the feel-good hormone serotonin, which accounts for most depressive symptoms known today.

DEPRESSION

Another report published by healthline.com shows that depression also affects the prefrontal cortex, the part of the brain responsible for emotion regulation, decision-making, and memory formation. When depressed, the body produces high amounts of the stress hormone cortisol. The excessive production of cortisol leads to the shrinking of the prefrontal cortex.

The third part of the brain affected by depression is the amygdala, the part of the brain that regulates emotional responses such as fear and pleasure. When one is depressed, the excessive release of cortisol leads to increased activity in the amygdala and its eventual enlargement.

Now that you understand what depression is and how it affects your brain, we will dive into the 21 secret ways you can use to overcome depression and live a depression-free life.

CHAPTER 2

10 Effective Ways to Care for Yourself and Overcome Depression

To ease or end depression, you can incorporate a number of simple yet powerful techniques into your life. In this section, we will discuss 10 proven and effective ways to combat depression:

1. Engage in Physical Exercises

Physical exercises are a natural remedy for a number of health-related issues, including depression. To beat depression, you can incorporate several exercises into your daily life. The ability for exercise to combat depression is drawn from the fact that, as you engage in physical exercise, your brain releases adequate and balanced amounts of endorphins. Endorphins are opioid neuropeptides that are the body's natural pain relievers. They act like opiates to relieve pain and induce feelings of pleasure and well-being. Whichever exercise you choose to engage in, practice it at least three times every week. For better results, dedicate at least 10 minutes to daily exercise. The great thing about exercises is that they do not just provide relief from depression; they also help you stay fit. The more fit you remain, the more positive you will be about life.

Adding mindfulness to whichever physical exercises you use to combat depression will further improve your results. Some common exercises you can mindfully employ to keep depression at bay include mindful walking, mindful jogging, mindful cycling, mindful swimming, mindful press-ups, etc.

Mindfulness is all about ensuring focused concentration on any activity you engage in at any given moment. To make your mindful physical exercises an effective depression remedy, follow this routine:

1. Relax and stop the flow of random thoughts into and out of your mind.

2. To slow your breathing, take slow deep breaths.

3. Concentrate on the movement of air into and out of your nostrils.

4. Pay attention to the sound the air makes as it goes in and out of your nostrils.

5. With each breath, observe your diaphragm up and down movements.

6. Begin the exercise and concentrate on how it affects your breathing and any other sound your body makes because of that particular exercise such as the sound of your feet

touching the floor while you run, the intensifying sound of your heartbeat as you complete your press-up or jogging, etc.

2. Eat Whole Unprocessed Foods

If you consistently neglect the importance of fueling your body with the right type of foods, you increasingly expose your body to attacks and invasions from different diseases that can keep you depressed. The unfortunate truth is that the age of technological advancements and proliferation of processed foods has made it more difficult to eat the right foods that ensure your body receives an adequate supply of the necessary nutrients. Today, it is easy to walk into any fast food and grab some tasty junk foods that are high in calories but lack adequate nutrients. There is a common saying: "You are what you eat". This saying emphasizes the need to eat well, which means eating more organic and natural foods that can help you stay in top shape.

A study by James E. Gangwisch, PhD. from Columbia University explored the link between depression and foods with a high glycemic index (GI). This is a scale used to rank carbohydrate-rich foods by how much it affects your blood sugar. His research team gathered data specifically on post-menopausal women. Seventy-thousand (70,000) women participated in this study, none of whom had a history of depressive disorders. Eventually, after three years of study, women whose diets were made up of foods ranked higher in the GI were more susceptible to depressive symptoms. In summary, this study concluded a strong link between depressive symptoms and added sugar.

DEPRESSION

Apart from nourishing your body and bolstering your immune system against diseases, eating healthy whole foods supplies your body with the energy it needs to fight stress, a known precursor to depression. When you eat the right foods, your brain also benefits. Basically, your diet can help you avoid certain factors identified as some of the major causes of depression.

Here are some useful tips to help you eat right and keep depression away for good:

1. **Insist on eating foods rich in brain-enriching nutrients:** The brain benefits from foods that contain loads of phytonutrients and antioxidants. Foods such as spinach, carrots, broccoli, and most leafy greens are great sources of antioxidants and phytonutrients.

2. **Eat plenty of vitamin and mineral-containing foods:** Foods such as vegetables, fruits, and other foods rich in vitamins and minerals keep your body nourished and improve your state of mind.

3. **Eat foods high in serotonin enhancers:** Serotonin is a happy hormone that helps you stay in a good mood and feel great. This is why you should get as much serotonin boosters as possible. Some foods raise the level of serotonin in your brain. Examples of such foods include fish and fish oils, foods rich in Omega-3 fatty acids, healthy fat sources such as coconut oil, avocado, eggs, chia seeds, flaxseed oil, etc.

3. Try Natural Supplements

A number of natural food supplements on the market today can act as antidepressants, improve your mood and energy levels, help you relax and get adequate sleep. These food supplements can help you get your life back on track after a bout of depression. These natural supplements work in the same way as antidepressant drugs prescribed by your physician when you are depressed. The only difference is that the natural supplements lack the side-effects commonly associated with many pharmaceutical anti-depressants. Whether you are already clinically depressed, or are simply trying to take preventive measures, natural supplements provide you with a natural antidepressant solution that helps your brain chemicals function at optimum levels, which helps you keep depression at bay.

Some popular natural supplements that can provide such antidepressant effects include fish oil, folic acid, melatonin, St. John's Wort, spirulina, maca and turmeric. Make sure you choose high quality, organic supplements. Avoid cheap synthetic supplements; they can cause more harm than good. If you are on any medications, it is advisable to check with your physician for guidelines on how to pair natural supplements with prescription medications. Most of these supplements come in powdered or liquid form. Thus, you can easily add them to your beverage or use them separately.

You will find more information on natural supplements in Chapter 6 of this book.

4. Eat Raw Dark Chocolate

Eating a moderate amount of raw dark chocolate can be a tasty way to feel good and lift your spirits when you feel less than excited or optimistic about life. You can make eating dark chocolate a part of your everyday routine. High quality raw dark chocolate is rich in antioxidants, alkaloids, beta-carotene, leucine, linoleic acid, lipase, lysine, and theobromine, all of which stimulate the nervous system, relax smooth muscles, and dilate blood vessels, giving the body a boost of energy and increasing circulation and availability of serotonin and other neurotransmitters in brain, improving mood and combating depression. Apart from improving your mood, eating dark chocolate can also boost your physical health and overall wellbeing.

It is important to eat dark chocolate in moderation if you want to ease depression. This is because eating too much of dark chocolate will make you feel bloated. Eating an ounce of dark chocolate daily is adequate to improve your mood.

5. Drink Organic Green Tea

In addition to containing a modest amount of caffeine, green tea contains other nutrients such as L-theanine, a nutrient that synergizes with the caffeine to sooth your mood.. This amino acid also helps alter the neurotransmitter levels in your brain, therefore producing more dopamine and serotonin that are known to positively affect a person's mood. Scientists have concluded that those who consume about four or more cups of organic green tea are 44 percent less likely to display symptoms of depression (in comparison to those who do not drink green tea daily). Green tea can also help reduce your stress levels due to certain anti-stress and anti-inflammatory compounds, boost your dopamine levels (the "feel good" hormone), and at the same time, increase your level of GABA, the brain inhibitory transmitter. All of this makes green tea a good natural way to fight depression

6. Replace Alcohol and Drugs with Fresh Organic Juices

When you are feeling depressed, alcohol and drug intake always seem like the easy way out. However, they will never help you overcome depression. Alcohol and drugs temporarily help you forget your problems, but the moment their effects wear off, you have to face the problems that caused the initial bout of depression. With time, the side effects of drugs and alcohol, and their addictive tendencies, will worsen your situation. Thus, instead of resorting to these substances seeking temporary relief, switch to the intake of supplements, green teas and fresh organic juices.

Researchers from the Otago Department of Human Nutrition decided to look up the link between a person's emotions and the food he or she consumes. The participants in the study were required to keep track of the food they eat during the evening, and record how they felt as soon as they wake up the next day. The results revealed that eating more fruits and vegetables the previous night resulted to feelings of calmness, happiness, and more energy the next morning. The recommendation is to eat antioxidant- and folate-rich foods to help lower the levels of homocysteine in the body.

Here are a few recommended organic juices that are beneficial to your overall well-being.

1. Green apple

Green apples are known to contain enzymes that promote a healthier digestive system. A healthier gut is known to help with depression as it clears the brain of fog and makes a person feeling healthier.

<u>RECIPE</u>

- 4 green apples – medium
- Celery – 4 ribs
- Kale – 12 big size
- Spinach
- Lemon

INSTRUCTIONS: Peel lemon and combine all ingredients in your blender or juicer. Once it's done, stir it well and chill before serving.

2. Spinach and cucumber

Spinach is known for its high vitamin and mineral content, as well as folate which is said to help regulate mood.

RECIPE

- Spinach
- Green apples – 2
- Cucumber
- Lime – keep the peel

INSTRUCTIONS: Leave the lime unpeeled and put all ingredients in your juicer.

3. Red cabbage

This is another key ingredient that's vital for healing the gut. As some studies suggest, a person with depressive symptoms would often find difficulty recovering if he or she has an unhealthy gut. Red cabbages are known to help with gut healing.

RECIPE

- Green apples – 2
- Carrots – 4
- Red cabbage – ¼
- Lemon
- Fresh ginger root – 1"

INSTRUCTIONS: Juice all the ingredients together and serve chilled.

4. Orange and Pomegranate

Pomegranate is known for packing a lot of antioxidants. On the other hand, orange contains bioflavonoids that boost the beneficial effect of antioxidants.

RECIPE

- Ripe pomegranates – 2
- Green apple
- Oranges – 2
- Lime – keep the peel

INSTRUCTIONS: Combine all ingredients in your juicer. Serve immediately. You can try keeping your fruits in your freezer so that they'll come out of your juicer chilled already.

7. *Get More Sunlight*

The sun has a therapeutic effect on your body. In fact, sunlight is a great mood enhancer. You know that natural feeling you experience when the early morning sun hits you? You experience this feeling because when you expose your body to more sunlight, your body produces more serotonin. Without enough exposure to sunlight, the serotonin level of the body lowers, which may lead to a higher risk of seasonal affective disorder (SAD)—a type of depression that gets triggered whenever seasons change. People who have SAD are prone to developing symptoms of depression during the winter season, in which the amount of sunlight is less. Other symptoms may include fatigue, difficulty concentrating, loss of interest in performing one's daily activities, excessive sleeping, and moodiness.

Get into the habit of getting more sunshine during the day by engaging in more outdoor activities such as running, jogging, walking, cycling, etc.

8. *Pamper Yourself*

Pampering yourself involves not being too hard on yourself, giving your mind and body adequate care, getting enough rest, etc. Below are several simple ways you can pamper yourself to deal with depression:

1. Go for regular massage or spa: Be good to yourself. One way to deal with depression is to pamper yourself with a regular massage or spa treatment. Both your mind and body do a lot to keep you going each day; therefore, it is important to give them adequate care so they keep serving you better. The more fit your body is, the less your chances of feeling the depression that comes from fatigue, stress, and incessant body aches. Scheduling a massage or spa treatment at least once per week will help you recharge and energize your body, which will leave less room for fatigue, stress, and depression.

2. Get help around the house: Apart from using regular massages and spa treatments to pamper yourself, you can also pamper yourself by hiring or getting someone to help you with doing various chores around the house. This will ensure you get some help and you do not feel overwhelmed and fatigued, which can easily lead to stress and probably depression.

3. Take a hot bath: A hot bath can help put you in the right frame of mind, a frame of mind that is free of worries. When combined with other techniques such as aromatherapy with burning fragrant candles and natural oils, a hot bath can provide you with the most soothing effect.

4. Occasionally prepare your favorite meal: Preparing the meal you love can be a good way to stay happy and in good spirits. Find the dish that tickles your fancy the most and occasionally prepare it as a way of treating yourself and making yourself feel great.

5. Cozy up with an interesting book: Sitting on the couch reading your favorite book can rejuvenate you and make you feel much better. Alain De Button — author of the books *How Proust Can Change Your Life* and *Religion for Atheists* — created a helpful, reading-related program together with his friends at the School of Life in London. The program, called "Bibliotheraphy", recommends a set of books for individuals who are struggling with their lives. A person receives his or her set of books to read after consulting with a bibliotherapist.

The idea behind the program is that reading offers people a way to distance themselves from their own troubles, and view their life through the perspectives of another's. Mostly, the stories are fictional, but the issues and themes prevalent in the stories are, in some way, relevant to the reader's troubles. This helps people see their depressive states through a new point of view, and the reading they do helps influence their brains into thinking that like the stories that they read, they will be able to move past their worries as well. This can effectively contribute a lot to their recovery from depression.

9. Get Adequate Sleep

Getting adequate sleep every night is one great way to maintain a positive mindset all through the day. If you have not been getting enough sleep, that could be one reason why you have been feeling more depressed lately.

When we talk of getting adequate sleep, some people think the more they sleep the better. This is not true: excess sleep also has its fair share of negative effects. When you get inadequate sleep or too much of it, it makes it hard for you to concentrate and stay positive during the day. Unhealthy sleeping habits can also usher in irritability, anxiety, and other depression-associated symptoms.

For best sleep benefits, experts advise the average adult to get 8 hours of sound sleep every night. Here are simple things you can do to sleep better at night:

1. **Keep your bedroom dark:** There is no magic to this one, just natural logic. When your bedroom remains illuminated during your bedtime, it tricks your mind into staying active. Your mind is likely to mistake the lights in your bedroom as daylight and thus stay awake for as long

as the lights stay on. Switching off all lights helps your mind deactivate and relax for sleep and a night of rest.

2. **Keep it quiet:** When you keep your bedroom as quiet as possible, you will enjoy better sleep. While some people might sleep better when they play some soulful music, most people sleep better when it is quiet. Thus, once you are ready to sleep, turn off the TV, turn off the radio, and turn off the music to help your mind concentrate on sleeping.

3. **Brew some chamomile tea:** Various teas like chamomile are very relaxing. According to some researchers, taking chamomile tea is associated with an increase in a chemical known as glycine that relaxes your muscles and nerves and acts as a sort of mild sedative. Thus, take some chamomile tea to sleep better.

It is also important to avoid things high in caffeine like coffee just before bedtime. This is because caffeine is a stimulant and taking it just before bedtime will stimulate rather than relax your mind, which is what you are looking for in order to fall asleep easily. Ensure you do not take drinks high in caffeine around 6 hours before bedtime.

10. *Balance Your Hormones*

Hormones are responsible for many bodily functions that can either leave us feeling healthy, happy and full of energy, or feeling flat, fatigued and unwell. Hormones are chemical messengers that are secreted by endocrine glands into the blood to then reach particular organs and tissues where they exert their effects. Our brains, adrenal glands, fat cells, ovaries and testes are the primary organs and cells that help to regulate and produce these hormones.

If your thyroid, adrenal or sex hormones are imbalanced, you may suffer from anxiety, depression, fatigue, food cravings, weight gain, poor libido or digestive problems.

See a good integrative medicine doctor and ask them to order and interpret the following tests:

- Thyroid gland tests - TSH, free T4, free T3, total T3, thyroid antibodies
- Adrenal gland tests - cortisol, DHEA-S, pregnenolone
- Sex hormone tests – estradiol, progesterone, free and total testosterone

More information on these in the chapter entitled "Overcoming Depression While Dealing with a Thyroid Condition."

Here is a list of foods that can help you balance your hormones naturally:

- *Oils*: Avocado, olive oil, coconut oil, flaxseed oil
- *Omega-3 Sources*: Wild Salmon and other low mercury fatty fish, flax seeds

- *Organic fruits*: grapefruit, lemon, lime, berries, kiwi, papaya, apples

- *Vegetables*: broccoli, cauliflower, kale, cabbage, collards, spinach, Swiss chard

- *Spices*: ginger, turmeric, thyme, rosemary, cayenne pepper, sage

- *Raw nuts and seeds*: almonds, pecans, walnuts, pumpkin, flax and hemp seeds

- *Legumes*: green beans, black beans, kidney beans chickpeas, quinoa

Incorporating these natural ways to take care of your body into your daily routine can boost your mood, help you improve your well-being, and keep depression at bay.

The next section deals with natural therapies you can use to deal with depression and stay depression free.

CHAPTER 3

Natural Therapies for Depression

This section deals with the natural therapies you can easily use to beat depression. The natural therapies we will look at are highly potent at fighting depression.

11. Meditation

Meditation is one of the greatest natural ways to cure depression. Most of time, we get so busy that we forget to find time to practice simple therapeutic techniques such as meditation, a practice that relaxes our minds and helps the body stay healthy, relaxed, and calm.

JAMA Internal Medicine — an international publication that features studies and information related to internal medicine — has analyzed 47 studies that point to the benefit of meditation when it comes to helping alleviate symptoms of anxiety, pain, and depression. John Hopkins School of Medicine's Dr. Madhav Goyal highlights the fact that even with as little as 2.5 hours of meditation a week, these benefits are still consistent.

DEPRESSION

Practicing meditation is not as hard as most beginners think it is. However, to get started, you do need some direction so you can get it right from the onset and maximize the benefits.

Below are simple steps to follow to practice meditation and overcome depression:

1. **Find a quiet place.** When your intention is to use meditation as a way to overcome depression, the first thing you must consider is finding a good place where you can enjoy complete quiet and concentration. As long as you remove every source of noise and distraction, anywhere can serve as a quiet place. For instance, if you decide to meditate in your bedroom, make it a quiet place suitable for meditation by turning off your mobile phone, TV, radio, locking your door, etc.

2. **Practice mindful breathing.** If you fail to regulate your breathing effectively, meditation cannot produce the desired results. Breathe in a slow and steady pace and concentrate on how the air moves in and out through your nostrils. Count the number of minutes each breath takes to complete, and notice the sound the air makes as it moves through your airways.

3. **Stop the random flow of thoughts.** Occasionally, rampant thoughts will invade your mind and try to steal your peace. You must stop the noise in your head generated by these random thoughts. You do not have to concentrate on not allowing thoughts into your mind—all you need to do

is acknowledge any thought that strays in and let it pass while keeping your concentration on your breath.

4. **Practice Gratitude.** Be grateful for all things that make your life easy and worth living, things you normally pay zero attention to. Think of how much it would cost you to breathe if you were to pay for each breath, and be grateful for this gift. Think of how wonderful life is and be grateful you have this gift. Focus on different parts of your body, one at a time, and feel grateful for all the ways each part of your body benefits your life.

Mindful meditation helps your mind return to a relaxed state where you do not dwell on the several issues that instigate stress and eventual depression. The longer you engage in mindful meditation, the less depressed you will feel.

12. Try Yoga

Technically, yoga is an exercise; however, the fact that it incorporates some mindful meditation technique gives it an added therapeutic effect. A number of yoga poses are effective depression remedies. When combined with mindfulness, these yoga poses can go a long way to help you relax and maintain a positive outlook on life.

Below are therapeutic yoga poses you can use to reduce, manage, and eventually overcome depression:

DEPRESSION

Head-to-Knee Pose (Janu Sirsasana)

This effective yoga pose helps you get rid of anxiety and depression. The effectiveness of this yoga pose lies in the fact that it stretches your entire body, including your shoulders, spine, hamstrings, etc.

1. Simply sit on your yoga mat, straighten your legs in front of you, and lower your head to your knees with your hands stretched in front of you.

Mountain Pose with Arms Overhead Pose (Urdhva Hastasana in Tadasana)

The mountain pose is a great warm-up posture. The vigorous upward movements your body experiences—from your limbs to your fingers, from your toes to your torso, and elsewhere—while you maintain the posture helps keep your system invigorated and your spirits lifted.

1. Simply assume the mountain pose with your feet placed hip distance apart.

2. Spread your arms above your head and stretch your fingers and toes.

3. Focus on the vigorous upward movements at your limbs and torso and breathe mindfully.

A combination of this pose and mindful breathing will help you eliminate depression because, when coupled with mindfulness breathing, this yoga pose invigorates your system and calms your nerves.

Bridge Pose (Setu Bandhasana)

This yoga pose is effective at relieving depression mainly because of its ability to calm your nervous system and relax your mind while strengthening your spine, neck, and hips.

1. Simply lie flat on your back and then lift yourself up with your feet and palms still on the ground.

2. Maintain the bridge position and breathe mindfully for at least 30 seconds to one minute.

The Corpse Pose (Savasana)

The corpse pose is rightly described as the most important yoga pose. Your yoga practice is never complete without the corpse pose. This pose helps you overcome depression by relaxing your entire body, calming your brain, and lifting your spirits.

1. Simply lie on your back, shut your eyes, and practice mindful breathing for at least 60 seconds.

2. The longer you stay in this position, the more the benefits you will derive from this pose.

13. *Use Light Therapy*

If your depression is seasonal, this therapy is ideal for you. Light therapy is also helpful to those experiencing major depressive disorder. Light therapy works by activating the circadian pacemaker in the brain responsible for sleep circle regulation. Since most sleep irregularities are linked to depression, light therapy is a beneficial way to normalize sleep disorders caused by depression.

The principle of light therapy has its working basis in the effect light has on brain chemicals, activating those chemicals to enhance sleep and improve your mood. Light therapy uses a light therapy box or a bright lamp (full spectrum that mimics natural sunlight). Simply sit and work near the box or lamp. A simpler way of doing this includes the use of a Dawn Simulator — a device that gradually increases the light in your bedroom during mornings, specifically when you are still slumbering. It may come in the form of a bedside lamp, which turns on gradually so that your retina would slowly begin to adjust to it long before you even open your eyes.

This particular therapy is seen as a potential antidepressant simply because the Dawn Simulator convinces your brain that it's still a sunny day, even when you are in the middle of winter. People are known to slow down naturally during the winter seasons, so doing this can help with simulating your brain, making it think that it's still summer. This can help prevent you from becoming lethargic.

14. Use the Color Combination Effect

Apart from the colors you wear, good color combination can apply to other aspects of your life. Learn which colors go together and which ones bring out the best and liveliest part of your mood. You know which colors get you smiling when you see them, and which ones turn you off the moment you lay eyes on them.

Painting the part of your home where you spend most of your time a happy color can be a great way to ensure you stay in the best mood all day and fell less depressed. Being around dull colors can contribute to a dull mood so make sure you go for cheerier, brighter colors that help you feel relaxed, calm, and excited.

People with anxiety and depression are often bound to associate their mood with the gray color, which is monotonous sand flat.. On the other hand, happier people are more likely to choose the color yellow. Here are some examples of colors and what they can do to help improve the mood in your home:

Red

The color red often raises energy, and is known to pump up the adrenaline more than any other color. It is also known to raise blood pressure, heart rate, and respiration speed.

Yellow

Yellow is known to communicate happiness and capture sunshine. Due to its energizing and uplifting property, it is a great choice for people with depression. However, it should not be used too excessively as large amounts of this color may create feelings of anger and frustration. This is probably because yellow is known to stimulate the nerves.

Blue

Blue is known to lower blood pressure, heart rate, and respiration speed (the opposite of red). It calms and relaxes, which is why it is often used to encourage relaxation in social areas of the home (e.g. living room, kitchen). Avoid choosing a shade that's too dark, because dark blues are known to have opposite effects and may also stimulate sadness.

Green

Green helps create harmony and balance. Most of the time, it creates a feeling of refreshment and calmness, and is also associated with good health, renewal, and positive growth.

Purple

Purple has always been associated with royalty, mystery, and creativity. Having the color purple at home is known to create a sense of being comfortable. Use a softer shade for a more calming effect as a too strong shade might create feelings of unease.

White

White has always been about purity, neutrality, and fresh beginnings. For most, white creates a sense of serenity and calmness that is, for the most part, relaxing. If you are the type of person who values cleanliness and serenity, then this color should go into your home.

15. Try Acupuncture

There have been a number of debates for and against the use of acupuncture as a way to treat mental disorders such as depression and anxiety. Nonetheless, acupuncture can be a beneficial way to ease and cure depression.

Acupuncture works by applying pressure on your body's pressure points; according to acupuncturists, your body has about 400 of these points. As soon as an acupuncture needle hits any of your body's acupuncture points, your body reacts by releasing a substantial amount of endorphins that give your body and mind a feeling of calmness, happiness, and relaxation.

This feeling continues long after the acupuncture session ends and, in the process, helps you get rid of depression. For better results, seek the help of a licensed and experienced acupuncturist to guide you through the process.

16. Go for Aromatherapy

Aromatherapy remains one of the most popular natural methods for treating depression. Aromatherapy uses essential oils extracted from flowers, herbs, and plants. These natural oils do not contain any trace of additives, chemicals, or preservatives. Some oils used in aromatherapy to treat depression include jasmine, lavender, and sandalwood.

Using aromatherapy to cure depression will require trial and error to find out what works best for you, although the above-mentioned essential oils are among the most commonly used. To

DEPRESSION

use these oils, simply inhale them and let their aromas circulate within your nostrils and lungs as they relax your mind and calm you. Essential oils' ability to relax your mood and bring your mental state to normalcy is what makes aromatherapy an effective way to treat depression.

By keeping you in high spirits, a combination of these natural therapeutic techniques will ensure you have less to worry or feel depressed about. The next section introduces several fun, natural activities you can adopt to make your life more fun and adventurous and keep depression at bay.

CHAPTER 4

6 Ways to Fun Away Depression

Living a boring life can easily lead to depression. One natural way to ease depression and its symptoms is to find ways to bring more fun into your life. Here are some natural ways to add spice up your daily routines:

17. Add Fun Activities to Your Life

Many people fill up their life with activities that do not add any value to life. Furthermore, filling your day with boring piles of work can easily get you depressed. However, adding one or two fun activities into your daily life can go a long way to help you stay depression-free.

When you incorporate fun activities into your daily life, it makes it easy to look forward to each day with enthusiasm and positivity. Here are some simple ways you can bring some fun into your daily life:

1. **Read an entertaining book:** The world has no shortage of entertaining books; find some and let them crack you up a little. You can borrow from your local library, buy from

DEPRESSION

your local bookshop or online bookseller, borrow from a friend, join a local reading club, etc. You can read joke books, fiction, poetry, plays, or anything that you know will make you happy.

2. **Watch your favorite sitcom on TV:** The sitcoms out there are too numerous to create an exhaustive list. There are TV channels that show only sitcoms and nothing else. When you feel low, find some of these channels and tune in to get some good laughs. Alternatively, you can follow some seasonal sitcoms on TV or online. YouTube equally offers you a wide range of choices of comic videos and programs.

3. **Go see a movie or comedy show:** Find a cinema center or a movie theater near you and spend time there watching a movie that interests you. You can go with someone you consider dear to boost the flow of your "feel good" hormones.

4. **Hang out with some funny and adventurous friends:** Your circle of friends undoubtedly has one or two friends who have a rare sense of humor that can get the most depressed person giggling and laughing as though he/she has no care in the world. To improve your mood, find a way to hang out with these people. You can invite them over for lunch, take them out to dinner, take them to a movie, invite them for a walk, etc.

18. *Find a New Hobby*

Never think it is too late to learn a new habit or pick up a new hobby. Having a hobby helps you have something that lifts your spirit whenever you remember it. Having a hobby you love so much to a point that it consumes you can help you channel your energies and live a more productive life. The hobbies you choose do not have to be something very taxing, like mountaineering or skating. All you need is something that helps you feel good and relax.

When deciding which hobby to pursue as a way to add more fun into your life and overcome depression, the important thing you must consider is how that particular task makes you feel. If it brings out a burst of energy and good mood, then that is the hobby you should stick with.

The hobby you choose should make you feel good before you engage in it, while you are engaged in it, and after you are done with it. The hobby you choose to use to beat depression should bring a smile to your face and a merry feeling to your heart each time you remember it or whenever the time to engage in it draws near.

When you learn to dedicate the free time you have during the day towards doing things that make you happy, you will have less time to think and worry about the things that make you depressed.

DEPRESSION

Here is a list of new hobbies you can easily adopt to deal with depression:

1. **Fall in love with music:** Loving music and falling in love with music are two different things. Falling in love with music will make you find time to be in an atmosphere where music is the lingua franca. You can join a local choir or music group for rehearsals, write a song, start practicing with your favorite music instrument, etc. It is not possible to be in love with music and still feel depressed. Music is a natural antidepressant.

2. **Become a writer:** Do not be one of those people who believe writing is for the gifted few. Anyone, including you, can become a great writer. If you can put your mind to it, writing can turn out to be your route of escape from depression. Write about anything, including your passions, your family, your love life, health issues, sports, music, politics, etc. The more you write, the better a writer you become, the better you become as a person, and the happier and less depressed you are bound to be.

3. **Develop interest in a new sport:** You can start playing football, basketball, table tennis, hockey, golf, etc. Find one sport you love watching others play and become one of the players so others can watch you play. New things bring new feelings of joy and accomplishment. Finding a new hobby like a sport can help you get rid of depression.

19. Accept Challenges and Try New Things

It is easier to shy away from challenges than it is to accept them. Sticking to the things your mind and body have become accustomed to will only make your life monotonous and boring. When you avoid trying new things, it is easy to feel discontented and depressed. To challenge your brain and make your life more exciting, take on challenging projects, especially things you have never tried before.

Challenging your brain with new tasks it is not used to engaging in is one way to ensure your brain never stops growing. However, when choosing new things and accepting new challenges, make sure you go for things you can do and not things you will fail at; choosing things you fail at will leave you feeling discouraged and feeling inadequate, which is what we are trying to avoid.

20. Plan Adventurous Trips with Friends and Family

One other way to spice things up in your life is to plan occasional adventurous trips with friends and family members. It is easy to feel bored when there is nothing exciting to look forward to. The adventures do not have to be things that put you and others at risk or things that can cost you your entire savings. Just organize a trip to the mountains, some game reserve, natural attractions like waterfalls, and rainforests and go for these trips with a few friends or your family. A simple road trip could be all you need to feel excited whenever you remember it.

DEPRESSION

21. Spend More Time Outdoors

It is easier for depression to set in when you spend more time indoors thinking about your challenges and ruminating over your difficulties than when you find ways to spend more time outdoors where you can enjoy the best of nature and interact with others.

The benefits of spending more time outdoors are numerous and far-reaching. They can range from enjoying more sunshine and its benefits, to getting more fresh air which can help you stay refreshed throughout the day. Finding time to get back to nature can be a great way to boost your mental health and overall wellbeing. Spending more time outdoors also helps you feel good about life irrespective of the activity you engage in while outdoors.

You do not have to limit your outdoor times to your morning workout periods. There are plenty of other ways to incorporate outdoor activities into your daily life.

Here are some simple ways to spend more time outdoors:

1. Take a walk in the park.

2. Go for a picnic.

3. Take your dog for a walk.

4. Play with your kids at the park or in your backyard.

22. *Get a Pet*

Pets can be the loveliest things to have around. Pets have the ability to help you feel good simply because pets make good companions. If you already own one, find time to devote to your pet. The more time you give to your pet, the more love you will receive from the pet.

If you do not have a pet, or you cannot get one for one reason or the other, you can go to a friend's house and play with their pet to experience the calming benefits. It is not possible to feel down or depressed while playing with a lovely and playful dog or cat.

CHAPTER 5

4 Rituals to Inspire Happiness in Times of Depression

Depression deprives us of one thing we need to really live a fulfilled life: happiness. Indeed, depression sucks the happiness out of people, taking out the excitement of living life to the fullest. Depression cripples a person's cognitive function, shatters their emotional health, and eventually takes a toll on a person's well-being.

If you are currently on the road to recovery, one thing you should focus on is to be happy. You might have heard one or all of your friends telling you to just "snap out of it" and just "be happy." As easy as it sounds to some people, to a person who is experiencing depression, it is one of the greatest challenges. It's a far longer road for them and, if anything, such words might only discourage them further.

Luckily there are daily practices that you can do which would help you develop the right state of mind. Alex Korb, PhD — a UCLA researcher specializing in neuroscience — identified four important rituals that can help inspire happiness to help people cope better with depression. Feel free to do these rituals if you need to give your happiness level a little boost.

Ritual Number 1: Ask yourself the most important question

Depressed people often find themselves hesitant to be happy. Maybe it's because they feel ashamed or guilty. Even so, there's actually a positive side to this, because believe it or not, feelings of shame and guilt actually activate the reward center of the brain.

In Dr. Korb's book entitled *"The Upward Spiral: Using Neuroscience to Reverse the Course of Depression, One Small Change at a Time,"* neural circuits located in the amygdala, nucleus accumbens, dorsomedial prefrontal cortex, and the insula become activated if a person feels either guilt, pride, or shame. This, in return, creates a satisfying feeling which is actually the brain's reward center turning on. Another similar feeling that creates the same satisfying feeling is worry.

Even though neuroscience has attested how guilt, worry, and shame create a sense of satisfaction in the human brain, these three are still not ideal as long-term solutions, especially for those who are dealing with depression. What you can do is to ask yourself the most important question, which is:

"What am I grateful for?"

Gratitude may sound too cliché, but what most of us may not be aware of is that it actually affects the brain at a biological level. Once again, Dr. Korb's book says that feelings of being grateful actually influences the part of our brain that produces dopamine. Whenever a person focuses on being grateful, this part of the brain becomes activated and produces more dopamine. On the other hand, when a person feels grateful to other people, the social dopamine circuits activate, thus making interacting with others more enjoyable.

Another benefit of gratitude is that it has been proven to boost the brain's serotonin levels. Thinking of things for which you are grateful motivates you to focus more on the positive aspects of life.

Asking yourself this important question does not come without a challenge, however, especially if the ill thoughts and feelings become a little too overwhelming for you to handle. If this happens, go to Ritual Number 2.

Ritual Number 2: Start labelling the bad feelings

For some people, giving the bad thoughts and ill feelings a name actually helps in their journey to recover from depression. A study was conducted on participants who were examined on using fMRI techniques. Each participant was shown photos of people with different facial expressions, which was found to activate their amygdala. However, when asked to give each expression a name (e.g. sad, angry, happy), the emotional reactivity from the amygdala decreased while the ventrolateral prefrontal cortex activated. This is scientific evidence that recognizing and acknowledging emotions has an impact on the brain.

In other words, suppressing emotions would only create suffering and does nothing when it comes to helping a person cope with depression. In fact, it may only worsen the symptoms. What helps is to give each bad feeling or emotion a name. You may use one or two words, adjectives, or any symbol you associate with a particular type of emotion. Labelling these emotions will also train your brain to become mindful, and will be useful should you decide to start meditating.

Ritual Number 3: Problem solving activities help you relax

Oddly enough, the brain is known to feel more at rest when a person engages in decision-making activities. We have all believed that doing activities that require problem-solving only causes stress, but science has proven otherwise.

The science of the brain shows that making decisions do not only help in solving problems but also reduces the symptoms of anxiety and depression. Decision-making positively engages the prefrontal cortex, which is the reason why anxiety and depression are calmed down. It has a significant impact on preventing striatum activities, which are known to draw a person towards routines and impulses that are considered negative. When making decisions, the body's limbic system relaxes, which actually helps you solve the problem at hand.

The decisions you make, however, should be "good enough." If you keep on insisting to reach 100% success in what you're doing, this will only stress you out even more. Note that being a perfectionist does not help in solving problems, but only prolongs the decision-making process and thus adds to your frustration. It also becomes a way for negative feelings to develop, making you feel worse about the situation and yourself. So try and be more lenient with yourself—you need not get everything right. Mistakes are totally fine. Imperfections? Even more so.

Relearning how to be content with simply having done your best for the day actually helps your brain relax, removing any lingering worries that come with always wanting to do things perfectly. The fact is, perfection is an impossible goal. The more you chase after it, the more stressed and depressed you can become. Keep this mindset when you're making decisions or solving problems—no one is keeping score. Just do what you can and that should be more than enough.

Ritual Number 4: Get in touch with people

The acceptance and love we receive from others play a huge role when it comes to our overall happiness. As human beings, we have this innate need to feel loved and accepted by the people we care about the most. Should we lack this in our life, feelings of inadequacy and abandonment might begin to develop. These feelings alone might cause depression in some people.

Another fMRI study shows that exclusion from social activities fires a signal in the brain that actually mimics the feeling of physical pain. In this study, the participants were asked to play a computer game where they were required to toss the ball to each other, without knowing that the other players were controlled by other people and not by a computer. Everyone was doing fine, giving each player a chance to catch the ball with every turn. However, as soon as they were told that they were, in fact, playing with other people, there were players who opted to pass the ball to one particular person repeatedly—in a way, ignoring everyone else still in the game. In those who were excluded from the game, their brain activity showed signals that were akin to that of someone experiencing feeling physical pain.

So, what does this teach us? It makes it clear that relationships have a vital role in supporting healthy brain activity. Another type of interaction that's beneficial to this would be the experience of physical touch. In fact, touching or simply hugging another person helps release oxytocin — also known as the "love hormone." Small affectionate gestures between friends and family are enough to induce this; for people who are in relationships, the effect tends to be greater as well. Touch, as you may have heard before, is a truly powerful thing and its influence on our brain shouldn't be underestimated.

If you have the opportunity to, hug the people you love and care for as often as you can. You may not think much of it, but in doing so, you're actually generating positive signals in your brain. The best part is that you're able to share that positivity with them as well. Aside from being effective in improving a person's state of mind, touch can also help make a person more persuasive. It also increases his or her performance in a group, and even helps boost their academic skills. It can aid in reducing pain, and even strengthens relationships. Did you know? Getting five big hugs daily and continuously for four weeks can produce a significantly positive effect on your happiness.

Summing It All Up

You have just learned about the four different ways through which you can boost happiness in your life using natural means. To recap everything, here's what you need to remember:

- To aid you in focusing more on the positive things in life, it helps to think of the things that you are grateful for each day. From the moment you wake up to the time you get to bed, thinking about these things will help you appreciate your life more.

- Each time you become overwhelmed with emotions, acknowledge it. Greet a negative feeling like you would an old friend. Give it a name. Only when you do not suppress a negative feeling will you be able to become free of it. However, do not linger on it. Acknowledge it and let it go.

- Start making goals and be firm when making the decision to pursue that goal. Try not to overthink a plan or pursue perfection when trying out something new. Everything is a learning experience — every mistake you make is a lesson and remember that you will grow from it. It is not a reason for sadness.

- Always make it a point to physically connect with the people you love. Sometimes, a hug is all you need to feel that everything will be okay and that you will surpass this challenge you are in right now.

Hey!

Hope you're enjoying this book so far. Please go to the link and leave a review on Amazon:

CHAPTER 6

Overcoming Depression While Dealing with a Thyroid Condition

Most people think that the only underlying causes of depression are life challenges, emotions, and feelings. However, many studies show that it could also be brought on by a thyroid condition. While earlier studies have found that women are more likely to be depressed than men, the case for linking depression with thyroid conditions is gaining ground thanks to numerous medical studies.

In 2002, research involving bipolar patients was able to point out that there were more thyroid antibodies in these patients than compared to the control group. This study was entitled "High Rate of Autoimmune Thyroiditis in Bipolar Disorder: Lack of Association with Lithium Exposure." Another study proved that the presence of these antibodies is not only prevalent in those with bipolar disorder, but also in those who are genetically prone to developing it. Furthermore, a 2004 study found that the presence of thyroid peroxidase antibodies (TPO Ab+) is linked with the development of mood and anxiety disorders. Lastly in 2005, a study involving subjects who had Hashimoto's disease —

a disease in which the thyroid gland is mistakenly attacked by the immune system — found that these subjects are more prone to displaying lifetime depressive symptoms, as well as social phobia, anxiety symptoms, and sleep disorders.

When a doctor meets a patient who has a thyroid condition, and is depressed at the same time, they are offered two different options for treatment. First, doctors provide medication to the patient in such a way that the amount of thyroid hormones in their body becomes normalized. Insufficient amounts of these hormones are usually the culprit that causes depression in these cases. Between synthetic and organic hormones, it is highly recommended to opt for the latter and use them with guidance from a holistic or a medical doctor. This would not only help with depression, but may also address other symptoms as well.

Another option that a doctor may provide is to prescribe the patient with an antidepressant. Although antidepressants are useful for addressing the urgent need of the patient, it actually does not do anything to treat the actual cause of the issue. While antidepressants might feel necessary at first, the most important thing in treating a patient is to get to the very core of their problem. Only then can they begin to recover from what is ailing them.

Natural Supplements: Do They Help with Depression?

There are certain natural and herbal supplements that are known to be beneficial for people with depression. Some people do not like taking prescription drugs due to the number of side effects, especially when there are alternative treatments which are just as effective—if not better, in some cases. However, this does not mean that there is no harm associated with natural supplements. There are still certain risks to keep in mind. It is for this reason that it's always a good idea to consult with a holistic doctor. There are instances wherein people who have severe depression may not respond well to natural or herbal supplements. If this is the situation that you or someone you love is facing, then prescription medication might be the better choice.

The following is a list of the supplements that are known to help with depression, whether or not a thyroid condition is also present.

5-HTP –Quite well-known for its capability to help with depression, 5-HTP is actually the precursor to serotonin — a chemical in the body that functions as a mood stabilizer. 5-HTP comes from the Griffona simplicifolia — an African plant. This is typically used as a treatment to help alleviate the symptoms from the following disorders:

- Anxiety
- Depression
- Insomnia
- Migraine
- Tension headaches

- Obesity

- Fibromyalgia

- Premenstrual syndrome (PMS)

When taking 5-HTP, you are actually stimulating your central nervous system, particularly the brain, to produce more serotonin. As a result, your appetite, sleep, sexual behavior, temperature, and even your sensativity to pain improves.

- **GABA** – This is another amino acid that's known to help stabilize moods by inducing calmness and relaxation. In fact, the absence of GABA — or Gamma-aminobutyric acid — may result in the following:

  o Lacking pleasure in life and its rewards.

  o Lack of concern for loved ones and other people without any apparent reason.

  o Decreased parental feelings.

  o No longer enjoying things that used to be "fun".

  o Decrease in spiritual and social life.

Do note that there are no studies yet that have linked GABA directly with depressive symptoms, nor is there evidence tying it to anxiety as well. What GABA does, however, is that it releases a relaxing effect on the brain, thus making a person feel less fearful and anxious after taking it. The bottom line here is that there is a naturally occurring link between GABA and depression, but there is little evidence that GABA has a direct effect on a person's mood. Nevertheless, the amount of GABA in the brain is still beneficial for stabilizing one's mood.

- **Omega 3 Fatty Acids** – Fatty acids are known to play an important role in maintaining the proper functioning of the brain. Although taking these alone will not help manage depression entirely, taking them with the other supplements mentioned in this chapter might certainly help significant changes.

According to the American Psychiatric Association, consuming adequate amounts of omega 3 fatty acids may just help in a person's fight against depression. In Norway, a study found that taking cod liver oil — which is rich in omega 3 fatty acids — daily can help lessen the chances of depressive symptoms by 30 percent. The longer you take cod liver oil, the less likely will you become affected by depression.

Omega 3 fatty acids, like GABA, also help in improving the mood of people with depression. At the Royal College of Surgeons in Ireland, a study was done on 49 patients who previously tried to harm themselves repeatedly. It was found that the group of patients who received omega 3 fatty acid supplements improved significantly compared to the other group who did not receive the same supplements.

Increasing the intake of omega 3 fatty acids enhances a lot of brain functions, including some aspects of personality and mood control. It also enhances one's cognitive processes, which increases one's attention span, therefore reducing symptoms of aggression. Needless to say, omega 3 fatty acids not only benefit the brain's overall functions, but can also influence depressive symptoms positively as long as it is taken regularly. The effects, of course, will not manifest overnight.

Eicosapentaenoic acid (EPA) is a type of omega 3 long-chain fatty acid that is sourced from fatty fish. It functions as a precursor to the formation of docosahexaenoic acid (DHA) — another omega 3 fatty acid that is present, largely, in the central nervous system. It is also found in the retina and the brain. EPA is a precursor to signaling molecules called eicosanoids which, according to the Inflammation Research Foundation, display anti-inflammatory properties that are vital for the treatment of major depressive disorder (MDD).

- **St. John's Wort** – For centuries, St. John's wort has been used for medical purpose in various parts of Europe and the United States. There has been quite a number of studies which prove effectiveness in treating depression, often comparing its effects to some popular antidepressants.

If you choose to use St. John's Wort as a way of treating your depressive symptoms, do be aware of the following side effects:

- o Increase in serotonin levels – Combining antidepressants with St. John's wort may cause a huge increase in serotonin levels, which may lead to a condition called the serotonin syndrome. This condition causes diarrhea and tremors, and severe cases can even involve stiffness of the muscles, confusion, drop in body temperature, and in some cases, death.

- St. John's Wort also weakens the therapeutic benefits of the following medications:

    - Antidepressants

    - HIV treatment drugs (e.g. indinavir)

    - Birth control pills

    - Digoxin (medication for the heart)

    - Some cancer treatment medication (e.g. irinotecan)

    - Cyclosporine (helps the body accept transplanted organs)

    - Blood-thinning medications (e.g. warfarin)

- Psychosis – This is a rare but possible side effect, especially with those who are highly prone to developing mental health disorders (e.g. bipolar disorder).

- Other side effects – Upset stomach, photosensitivity, may worsen anxiety symptoms.

Other things to consider when using this supplement is to never postpone an appointment with your doctor. Note that depression symptoms, when inadequately treated, may become severe and might only cause a myriad of other problems. Keep in mind that when using this herb you should follow the correct dosage and make sure you avoid any negative interactions with other medications or supplements.

- **Tryptophan** – Another serotonin-stimulating amino acid, tryptophan is also a neurotransmitter that can help relieve the symptoms of depression. However, just like the St. John's Wort, it comes with a few risk factors that you must consider before taking it.

Note that you cannot take tryptophan together with selective serotonin reuptake inhibitors (SSRIs) for the interaction between the two could bring about negative side effects. Always be honest with your doctor about what other supplements you are taking so they would be able to avoid prescribing medication that might interact negatively with it.

Getting to the Heart of the Problem

The key to overcoming depression completely is to not rely on medications or supplements, especially if you have a thyroid condition. Both nutritional supplements and prescription medication can help manage the depressive symptoms, but the main goal should always be to treat the underlying cause. As mentioned earlier in this chapter, people with thyroid conditions who are taking a synthetic form of thyroid hormone would need

DEPRESSION

to switch to a natural form, or add T3 under the guidance of a licensed doctor.

Also mentioned is the fact that people with thyroid problems have a tendency to develop depression. This may be because the thyroid hormone in the body is imbalanced, so the goal here is to pinpoint which areas contain the imbalance to be able to address them directly.

Natural treatment methods for the thyroid have helped many people with depression. For people who are diagnosed with thyroid hormone imbalance, a natural treatment protocol would be ideal to help restore the thyroid's normal function. However, natural treatments do not work on all people, but they do for some.

Aside from the thyroid hormone, there may be other hormones that could cause this particular issue. Cortisol imbalance, for example, is also known to cause depression due to the imbalance of the sex hormones — both for males and females. To determine this, the patient would be required to go through a hormone panel and/or an Adrenal Stress Index to detect which hormones are imbalanced. Not all doctors perform these tests, however; some may just administer treatment for the thyroid hormone right away and see how it might affect the patient. Only when the symptoms persist will they decide to conduct other tests.

Note that different doctors have different approaches when it comes to this, and some might choose to address the depressive symptoms right away. One thing they will not do, however, is advise their patients to abruptly stop their medication, as it is not required to do so before beginning with natural treatment protocols. Doctors will usually wean their patients off the medication carefully and slowly, under their close supervision.

In summary, depression that happens as a result of a thyroid condition can be managed through prescribed medication, and even through the use of natural supplements. But just like any other condition, the main goal should always be to treat the core of the issue, which in this case is the thyroid problem. Once thyroid function is restored back to normal, any other hormonal imbalance may be treated, including depression.

CHAPTER 7

Dealing with Stress and Depression

People who are battling with depression often feel like the world is overwhelming and highly stressful. The very thought of overcoming depression, in itself, is already a huge source of stress—which can sometimes lead to the person delaying treatment, thinking that going through the process would only cause them further frustration. A depressed person can also lack proper motivation, as well as the strength that they would need to overcome the challenges that come with treating the problem.

In this chapter, we'll examine a number of different strategies for managing stress as well as depression. These are the tips shared by 30-year life coach Tony Robbins, a man whose work has managed to help change many people's lives.

1. Decide to live in a beautiful state: Most of the people who are diagnosed with depression often have a negative view of their current life. It may be normal for a person to feel overwhelmed at what life is throwing at them, but if you keep using this as an excuse for everything, the result will be heaps of stress. Tony

Robbins believes that this is not so much about how life presents itself to people, rather how people react to it.

How you perceive your life says a lot about your habits, your outlook, and the language that you speak. Describing life negatively, using negative adjectives and words, works like a mantra — repeat them every day and soon enough, you'll be internalizing these negative things.

What you can do is to train yourself physically to live in a beautiful state. Repeatedly thinking that you are stressed would therefore train your mind to think that stressing out is the appropriate reaction you should give to any difficult situation. If you train yourself to feel and believe as though life is beginning to drowning you, then eventually it will.

The thing is, you do not have to think about how stressful things are! Think about your passion, your positivity, and your strength. The idea here is to never settle for negative habits that do not help you become better. Instead, push yourself to think that you are better than all the negativity surrounding you and that you need to get up and start changing the way you see your life.

One way to make this easier is to find something that makes you enjoy life. Something to live for, so to speak. Do it for yourself or do it for a loved one. What's important is that you find that spark of energy inside yourself that can get you motivated. Always keep in mind that life is indeed too short, and there will be mishaps along the way. However, choose not to wallow in those things and learn how to move on, and to see the beautiful in everything.

2. Raise your standards: The thing with motivation is that it is a bit tricky. Where exactly do your motivations lie? Why are you doing what you are doing? Are you doing this simply because you need to, or because you really want to?

In this second step, Tony Robbins encourages people to know their "Why." *Why are you working? Why are you saving up? Why are you doing this for your family? Why do you love?* These are some of the questions that would help you find a reason to keep pushing forward and continue what it is that you're doing. It may feel like a huge, solid wall at first, but eventually, you will be able to discover what ignites that spark and really gets you going.

If, for example, you find it an absolutely impossible task to try to find your "Why," Tony Robbins encourages people to be around others who appear to have found their "Why." Watch interviews, read the news, and read autobiographies of people you admire. Learn about their beginnings and how the result of their passions was able to turn their lives around completely. By looking at these things, not only can you gain inspiration from it, but you'll also gain perspective on what your life might be lacking at the moment. This is the time when you might begin to make changes, realizing that you need to raise your standards and never settle.

3. Better yourself: Tony Robbins believes that the quality of your life also depends on your emotional state. However, changing one's emotional state can be very challenging, and some people tend to give up before even trying. But, if you do that, how will you recover? How will you better yourself? Here are some tips to help you get started.

- Feed your mind 30 minutes a day.

Tony shares that back when he was homeless, he lacked the access to the internet and, as such, didn't have the same liberty we do now to learn new things through it. This doesn't mean that he gave up completely, though. What he had was a strong desire to feed his mind with information, and for this, he went to the local library and started reading as many books as he could.

Feed your mind 30 minutes a day with information and skills you want to learn. It doesn't matter how mundane it might seem — this counts as effort towards becoming better. Those 30 minutes a day might not feel like much at first, but eventually, these 30-minute sessions will help strengthen and train your mind to become better through consistent effort.

- Strengthen your body.

Most people fear change, and fear often affects the body's physical state. It has been mentioned over and over in this book that exercise does your body good, especially when dealing with emotional and mental health challenges such as depression. Running, walking, and jogging helps train not only the physical body, but eventually the mind will catch up as well. Fear is known to change the body's biochemistry in a negative way, so by strengthening your body, you're also giving it a better chance to defend against any physical effects that fear might trigger. After all, if you feel strong, the mind is bound to follow that same line of thought.

- Find a mission bigger than yourself.

Find something that you are willing to work for even though there will be huge challenges along the way. The idea here is similar to what Tony has shared about raising one's standards — you have to determine the purpose behind what you are doing, even if there are a lot of challenges along the way. In other words, find your passion and your passion will lead you to where you should be.

- Find a role model.

Yes, you read it right; the fourth key strategy towards making yourself better is to look for someone to look up to. Having a role model makes your dreams and aspirations real enough. Having a role model will also keep you motivated, and will help inspire you to strive better to achieve your dreams.

- Remember that there are people who are worse off than you are.

Putting your life into perspective can be challenging, especially if all you have done recently is view your life negatively and think that life only sends you insurmountable challenges. Before you begin your tirade of miseries, remember that there is always another person out there who might be experiencing the same things, only threefold. No matter how successful you are, it is always important to keep your life as meaningful as you can by making sure you contribute to the life of others even in simple ways such as giving encouragement and compliments. In giving back, not only do you better yourself, but you help others do the same as well.

4. Believe that you can do things, and start taking action: Depression is known to suck the optimism out of people. It is understandable if you end up losing your drive to work on your goals and dreams if you are struggling to overcome depression.

Tony Robbins encourages people to train their minds, to make it believe that they are capable of achieving the results they want. With this belief, your mind goes into action mode—enabling you to really strive for what it is that you want. This, however, does come with its own set of challenges. The biggest obstacle is not something that's in your environment. It's in your head. If you start believing that you cannot do it, then everything else follows that way of thinking.

What you can do is to write down your potential goals: the ones you're clear on and the others that may need further development. Take a moment to reflect on them. Think of the steps that you can do to maximize your potentials. It doesn't matter how small the step is or how much time it might take you to get there, what counts is that you're putting in an effort. Believe and work on things.

Note that every potential is extraordinary, and that whether or not you tap into a potential has to do with how much action you are willing to take. The action you dedicate towards that potential will determine the results. People with little beliefs will take little action, and this will greatly affect the results.

Training your mind to feel comfortable despite any uncertainty will make you believe that there's a lot of potential in every situation. This will further encourage you to take the necessary MASSIVE action which then becomes the key towards great results. What happens as a product of all this is that your belief in your own self will be strengthened and, with that, your ability to achieve goals grows as well.

Depressed people believe that the future for them is dark, therefore eliminating the potential that things will turn out better in the end. This is why the "believe" mindset is an ideal training exercise for the mind; if you believe that you can surpass your depression, then you will surpass your depression.

5. Find meaning in your life: One thing that often reduces people to thinking that there is no purpose in their lives is the monotony of everyday living. *Why am I working? Why am I saving up?* While you may readily answer that you are doing what you are doing so that you will attain financial stability, using that as your sole goal in life defeats the overall purpose of living. In the end, you will find that money matters very little if you want to live up to your full potential. Finding meaning in what you do and in your life, gives you a clearer picture of what you want—it also boosts your motivation, because now you have something to really strive for.

In trying to find meaning in your life, it's best to do it slowly. Get into the habit of listing down things that give you joy and make you feel fulfilled. What are some of your passions? When do you feel most satisfied about your life and the work that you do? These are simple questions, but the answers you give to them can provide insight into finding your meaning. Remember, do not rush. Give it time and eventually, the answer will come to you. Enjoy the process as you go.

The thing with stress is that it isn't something you can simply turn your back on and forget. This is especially true for people who are trying to overcome depression—the task of "eliminating" stress is a much harder challenge for the mind that doesn't exactly bend according to how we want it to. That said, a challenge can still be surpassed; it takes time and confidence in yourself. Confidence which you will need to build slowly but surely. Practice the given steps and be consistent, and eventually, you'll start seeing and feeling the positive changes they bring.

CHAPTER 8

Dr. Ilardi's Therapeutic Lifestyle Change for Depression

Despite the huge increase in antidepressant use, the number of people diagnosed with clinical depression continues to rise. Today, depression continues to be among the top reasons for work-related disability for people aged 50 and below. In spite of this, previous studies have provided evidence to suggest that depression can now be treated and prevented by simply changing one's lifestyle. In fact, Dr. Stephen Ilardi, PhD — associate professor from the Department of Psychology at the University of Kansas — headed a research unit that revealed how therapeutic lifestyle changes (TLC) were able to help about 70 percent of the respondents reduce their depressive symptoms by at least half.

Elements of the TLC for Depression

When it comes to treating depression, it is often not enough to rely entirely on medication to relieve the symptoms. For this reason, Dr. Ilardi formulated the following essential elements for

TLC, which could help in further improving a person's chances of getting well and surviving depression.

- **Omega 3 Fatty Acids:** As discussed earlier in this book, infusing Omega 3 fatty acids into one's everyday diet can help with significantly decreasing depressive symptoms. Studies show that these fatty acids are also important in improving the dopamine and serotonin circuits in the brain to help it function more efficiently. Omega 3 fatty acids may come in supplement form and can be bought from health food stores or drugstores.

- **Exercise:** The benefits of exercise not only include becoming fit and healthy, but are also known to decrease the likelihood of depressive symptoms getting worse. Although exercise is beneficial for recovery, it is also one of the most challenging, since not everyone will be as motivated as others to get started. It takes up time and energy, but the effort you put into it certainly provides results. Even a quick workout can easily boost a person's mood and give them more energy for the day. It's an all-natural alternative to antidepressant, one that you can do each time you feel the need to.

The most effective exercise schedule should last about 30-40 minutes and should be done three times a week. Start off with something simple yet effective, such as aerobic exercise (e.g. running, brisk walking, basketball, biking). This is great for elevating the heart rate. On the other hand, anaerobic exercises (weightlifting, yoga) may also be useful if you have a condition that might hinder you from performing aerobic exercises.

- **Anti-Rumination Strategies:** Way back in time, people always had so much to do, staying on their feet in their attempt to finish the day's work. This didn't leave much room for sitting down and pondering negative thoughts. However, these days there's a lot of room for rumination, and while this can be good in moderation, too much of it can be quite unhealthy.

The Merriam-Webster dictionary defines rumination as "to go over in the mind repeatedly and often causally or slowly." Such a habit can be destructive, especially if the thoughts a person tends to repeatedly think are negative—such is the case with many people who are going through depression. Think of it as the complete opposite of daydreaming, which a harmless habit that brings to mind positive images. Can you imagine repeatedly going through all of the mistakes you have made in the past? Constantly obsessing over what you could have done? Not only is it fruitless, it is also mentally damaging.

Rumination also comes with a number of harmful side effects. Below are a few examples:

- o There are many cases wherein people resort to binge-eating as a way to block out their ruminations. This has been proven in a study conducted by Susan Nolen-Hoeksema, PhD of Yale University. While food is relatively harmless, too much of it can actually bring about imbalances in the chemical make-up of both the body and brain, which can cause the symptom to worsen.

- o If not dealt with accordingly, rumination can become a habitual cycle and does little to help people recover from depression. Dr. Nolen-Hoeksema concluded in her study that rumination coupled with ill feelings can double the effects of depression in most people. It can produce a bleak picture of their current situation, leading them down a path of negative thoughts.

- o People who ruminate have a higher chance of developing feelings of helplessness and weakness. One particular effect of this is that it diminishes a person's ability to solve problems. He or she becomes so engrossed with the problem that instead of finding a solution for it, they end up drowning in it. As much as possible, this is something people with depression must avoid.

- o Obsessive rumination can actually begin to isolate people from others. They can end up pushing their loved ones away when they fall deep into the negative space they're in. This causes frustration in both parties, and the last thing that a depressed person needs is to find themselves alone.

- **People/Social Support:** Even if you're the type of person who craves solitude, it is important to connect with other people, whether it be with your friends or your close family members. However, as a person sinks deeper into depression, they become less and less inclined to build these relationships with other people. They begin to withdraw from socializing, whether it be out of shame or guilt over the frustrations they believe they're causing to others. This is very detrimental towards their recovery. The point here is that spending time with your loved ones and rebuilding those strained connections will be beneficial. You will need people you can lean on and talk to whenever needed—instead of internalizing all your feelings, having someone to confide in will certainly help. Allow these people who truly care for you to support your journey. The first step is opening yourself up to them.

- **Exposure to Light:** Studies show that in some instances, depression can have a seasonal component. Basically, if the sun is shining brightly, then this affects your mood positively. However, if the weather is gloomy and dull, then your emotions may reflect the same.

Try to establish a schedule that allows you to enjoy sunlight or any source of good light whenever you're doing something. Most people like having their breakfast by a window, while others like being near a lightbox at night while they read or study. Consistency here is the key, so make sure you stick to your schedule to get the maximum benefits.

- **Sleep Hygiene:** Due to the world becoming more and more demanding in terms of work, many see sleep as something expendable. Most people choose to sleep less and less as long as there is extra work or studying to be done. Watching a late-night TV show is no exception. In fact, this has become one of the main reasons as to why some people get very little rest.

Although the amount of sleep need by different people tends to vary, it is important to try and get an average of 8 hours of sleep every night. Sleep deprivation is an acute or chronic condition which results to daytime sleepiness, fatigue, weight gain or loss, and may cause adverse effects to a person's overall cognitive function. If a person lacks sleep, they become much more irritable and prone to bouts of depression throughout the day—needless to say, this is something one should really avoid.

For a healthier sleep pattern, try doing the following:

- o Try to set a daily schedule for going to sleep and waking up. Make sure that you stick to it. Make going to bed at 10 PM and waking up at 6 AM the next day a habit. Even if you're not sleepy, do things that would tire you out so when the hour comes, your body itself would demand rest. Try to complete at least eight hours of sleep each night.

- o Have a bedtime ritual. You may light a scented candle, read a book, and avoid anything that gives off a blue light (e.g. mobile phones, laptop screens, TVs), put on your most comfortable pajamas, and stay in bed. You can even make use of aromatherapy which is a great way to naturally induce sleep.

- o Avoid drinking anything that contains alcohol and caffeine within 3 hours before your bedtime. Caffeine will only keep you awake, while alcohol will alter your state of mind in a way that would make it difficult for you to catch your Z's.

What Dr. Ilardi has shared above should not be mistaken as the sole treatment for depression. It is basically a way of changing your habits into something that aids your recovery from depression. What we do on a daily basis greatly affects our state of mind, and though we pay little attention to it, even the smallest things have an influence over how we feel or how we think. The overall objective is not only to treat depressive symptoms, but also to improve one's well-being as treatment continues.

CHAPTER 9

One Day at a Time: The 24-Hour Guide to Survive Depression

Douglas Bloch — teacher, author, and mental health coach who is also a depression survivor — shares that during his journey, he discovered that the best way to cope with severe depression is to try and live one day at a time. Doing so helps us arrive at a point where we contemplate about the pain without being overwhelmed by everything else. Studies have shown that living one's life in 24-hour segments is proven to be more manageable, especially for people who are depressed and are going through a rough time.

In this chapter, you will learn how to create a daily survival plan to better cope with depression. It helps to live through each hour, every minute, and even seconds. Creating your own personal survival plan can be effectively done by taking four (4) different strategies into consideration:

- Physical support

- Mental/emotional support

- Spiritual support

- People support

Physical Support

As the name implies, physical support is all about nurturing one's physical body. To do this, the following elements should be considered.

1. **Exercise:** As we have established, getting active does significant good to the physical and mental body. Many studies over time have proven that exercise does have a positive effect to one's mood; stabilizing and elevating it, therefore contributing to overall health. A healthy body makes for a healthy mind.

2. **Diet and Nutrition:** When it comes to providing your body with the right nutrients, protein and complex carbohydrates are the most ideal if you are currently dealing with depression. As much as possible, steer clear of simple sugars because it highly affects the overall emotional state of the body.

3. **Medication:** Any prescription medication should be taken on a regular basis and as prescribed by the doctor. If you are planning to stop taking your medication or changing your dosage, do so onlu after you have consulted with your doctor so you will not suffer any side effects afterwards. Never decide these things for yourself—

remember that any imbalances in your chemical make-up can have adverse side effects.

4. **Sleep:** Setting a regular sleep schedule will help your body properly recharge. It will also allow you to set a routine, something very important for people who are going through depression. The easier sleep comes to you, the more rested and energetic you feel the next day.

- Prep the environment.

Turn of all the lights and bring out your bedtime aromatherapy kit. You can opt to light lavender scented incense, as it is known to induce relaxation in both mind and body. Make sure your bed is inviting and that the room itself is properly ventilated—not too hot or too cold. Keep your surroundings clean and free of disturbing clutter so your mind does not stray from what it's supposed to be doing which is resting.

- Drink chamomile tea before bedtime.

Chamomile tea is popular for its relaxing and soothing effects. If you need to drink something before bed, make sure it is something relaxing like this tea. Avoid highly caffeinated drinks or anything that's high in sugar content.

Emotional/Mental Support

People who are clinically depressed tend to become overwhelmed with a lot of feelings and thoughts. Due to these thoughts and feelings, the brain overworks itself and triggers neurochemical changes. This is what causes symptoms to appear, such as those of anxiety and depression. To relieve your depression symptoms, an effective coping strategy is to closely monitor how you think and feel about things. Here's how:

1. Monitoring self-talk: In cognitive-behavioral therapy, monitoring self-talk is one of the most integral strategies used. Often times, people who are diagnosed with depression have little to no control over their thoughts and typically find this part challenging, especially if done on their own.

The overall aim of monitoring self-talk is to see how kindly we speak to ourselves. Is it positive? Negative? Do we have a tendency to bring ourselves down? If so, monitoring your self-talk enables you to correct these things and inject more positive affirmations that would boost our motivation. It's a simple habit, but it does help heal the mind.

2. Practicing self-compassion: People who have depression would usually experience feelings of shame, blaming themselves or feeling guilty for their mistakes. When depressed, it is often helpful to remember that going through depression is like battling with an illness, and that you are not at fault. Your depression is not caused by personal weaknesses, nor is it caused by a defect in character. You have to remind yourself that there is nothing wrong with you and that you have the power to turn things around. There's no rush in doing so, however. Work on things at your own pace and make sure you congratulate yourself for even the smallest of efforts that you do. Each thing counts!

3. **Keeping a mood diary:** Some psychiatrists require their patients who are depressed to keep a daily diary in which they to log their current moods. Creating a daily mood scale involves the simple act of monitoring and observing moods, as well as their triggers. This is not only useful for keeping track of emotional changes, but it allows people to see how medication might be affecting how they feel.

Below is an example of a daily mood scale.

	Happy	Sad	Tired	Excited	Anxious	Other	Notes
6 AM – 8 AM							
8 AM – 10 AM							
10 AM – 12 PM							
12 PM – 2 PM							
2 PM – 4 PM							
4 PM – 6 PM							
6 PM – 8 PM							

Aside from these mood scales, there are other easier ways to track one's moods. In fact, there are apps such as Daylio and Moodtrack Diary which have been designed specifically for this purpose. Do take advantage of these things! It would provide you with great insight when it comes to your own self.

4. Reciting affirmations: Think of these as mantras. They are inspiring phrases that you repeatedly tell yourself whenever you start feeling down. The repetition helps you calm down and can even help with keeping your heartbeat at a steady rate—helpful if you're feeling anxious. Add the note of positivity and you can boost how you feel as well, giving you that extra bit of confidence you might need to get through certain difficulties.

Here are a few examples of affirmations:

- *"Today, I am overflowing with happiness and brimming with energy!"*

- *"I am the boss; my emotions shall not win over me!"*

- *"Today, I choose happiness, and happiness chooses me!"*

- *"I am brave, courageous, smart, and worth anyone's time!"*

- *"This time, I am abandoning my harmful habits and taking up positive ones!"*

5. Being more aware and thankful for the small things: The quality of life is not measured with the numerous achievements that you may or may not have. It's all in the small things, the details. A kind word from someone you admire, a hug or encouragement from people that you love. Having the ability to spend time with friends, laughing and simply being in the moment. The often intangible things that we tend to overlook are also the most important. Once you begin seeing them in everything, even in the challenges, you'll start noticing changes in how you perceive things. It really give you a brighter, more positive outlook in life.

Spiritual Support

Most people draw strength from their faith, and most depression survivors have listed faith among the top reasons for their recovery. Spirituality can play a crucial role in helping people pull themselves out of depression, but of course, this does not apply to everyone. If you highly value spirituality, then by all means, embrace it!

Faith helps people sit down with their depression and examine it on a deeper level. This process of self-introspection, meditation, and reflection helps people find something to live for, allowing them to realize that there's more to life than just the daily struggles we experience. In fact, at least 444 studies are known to have quantitatively examined the relationship between depression and religious/spiritual (R/S) involvement. Over 60 percent of these reports show the decrease in severity of depressive symptoms from people who are more involved in R/S activities (Bonelli, Dew, Koenig, Rosmarin & Vasegh, 2012).

If you want to get in touch with your spiritual side to help you cope with depression, here is how you can do so:

1. **Improve your faith:** Your relationship with your faith is a deeply personal one, and will help you look into your inner self at a deeper level. Meditation or attending

spirituality workshops are only a few examples of how you can get in touch with your faith.

2. **Talk to a spiritual advisor:** If, for example, you feel like you can't do it on your own, you can always seek help from a spiritual advisor that you trust. Spiritual advisors are there to help people who are lost get back on track with their faith. If you do not feel comfortable talking to someone in your family, or even a close friend (as you feel they might be biased in opinion), this is another option you can turn to.

3. **Ask others to pray with you or for you:** If prayer is of utmost importance to you, then ask the people you love to help you cope with your depression either by praying with you, or praying for you. Your faith in prayer and the fact that you're aware of people personally supporting your journey to recovering can certainly heighten feelings of confidence and love within you—two very important things when it comes to dealing and overcoming depression.

4. **Make your intentions clear:** With everything you do, always have clear intentions. Write out what it is that you want to achieve through meditation or the other spiritual practices that you're working on. Keep these intentions in mind as you continue on; not only will they help you stay on the right track, they will enable you to see just how far you've come.

People Support

Yes, depression can turn people into hermits. But it is important that you make an effort towards social interaction. Ease yourself into socializing—it will really help your mental state and enable you to avoid internalizing too much.

1. Arrange your daily schedule: Make plans so that you'll be able to spend a bit more time with your loved ones throughout the day. If your children leave early in the morning to go to school, wake up an hour earlier so you can have the chance to interact with them before they leave. If your best friend goes to yoga class on Saturdays, but you do not feel like being in a class with that many people, talk to them about scheduling classes for just the two of you.

Spending time with people you care for activates parts of the brain that induces good feelings. So that brunch with friends you're planning on skipping out on? Attend it. Get dressed, make yourself feel good, and enjoy their company!

2. Attend group therapies or depression support groups: Support groups are a great way to meet people who are going through a similar experience. Draw inspiration from these people and learn from them as well. This is a place where you can offer support to other people, too, enabling you to see your situation from more than just your own perspective. This is very helpful.

If after your support group discussions you still feel the need to talk to somebody, websites such as DailyStrength are safe spaces

DEPRESSION

on the Internet to post about your worries and where you can get people to reply to you. Sometimes getting affirmations from people who you do not know personally may just be what you are looking for on the road towards recovery.

Although these factors are known to help, it does not mean that these are the only things you'll need for your recovery. True enough, there is no such thing as a one-size-fits-all strategy to recover from depression. You, as a budding survivor, and these strategies are part of the process to getting through the tough times you're experiencing right now.

No matter how bad things seem, remember that what's truly important is focusing on the present. On making yourself feel okay in the "now". Concentrate on living your life one day at a time and do not stress yourself out fearing what could happen in the future. Remember that the only constant thing in the universe is change, and that whatever struggles you have today will pass.

Creating a daily plan for yourself will not only help you get things done, but will also give you a way to track your thoughts and feelings. Plan out what you want to do for the day, and in between those, schedule things that would help you manage the symptoms of depression. Consider the suggestions above in doing so—remember, it need not be a huge step. Even the smallest ones still matter and can be considered progress.

CHAPTER 10

Inspirational People and How They Overcame Depression

It may not seem like it, but there are a number of iconic people who battled depression before and managed to come out on top. In this chapter, you will learn more about them and their stories which might help inspire you to continue pushing forward with your own journey towards recovery.

3 Historical Icons

When we think of history's many significant characters, we mostly only remember their achievements they made. Little is talked about when it comes to the other, quieter battles they may have faced.

Abraham Lincoln

Yes, our dear Abe had it, too. Joshua Wolf Shenk — biographer and author of *Lincoln's Melancholy: How Depression Challenged the President and Fueled His Greatness* — wrote about Abe's depressive breakdowns when he was 26 and 31 years old. According to records, Abe's statement often contained hints of suicide, causing concern among his friends, making them go as far as putting him on a suicide watch.

But Abraham, despite his condition, was still able to boost the morale of those around him through the use of humor. This is what served as a distraction for him as well and allowed him to connect better with people. In time, as we all know by now, he was able to overcome his depression and used that very problem to fuel himself when it came to achieving his goals.

Sigmund Freud

One historical icon that has contributed a lot to analyzing the human mind is Sigmund Freud. "Libido," "denial," "Freudian slip;" all of these terms would not be around if it were not for Freud's eccentric mind. Being an icon in the field of psychology, who would have thought that he, too, suffered from periodic depression, even anxiety attacks?

One of his attempts to overcome depression was to use cocaine. For him, it was a success, as he was able to control himself to take only small doses. However, this led to overuse; not wanting to further disappoint the people around him, Freud discontinued using it.

He was able to eventually get past his depression when his work began gaining recognition from the world. Freud's work involving dreams, psychoanalysis, and sexuality was received well all over the world, and many people looked up to him as a leader. This fame of his became the antidote for depression.

Siddhartha Gautama

Before he became Buddha, he was Siddhartha. He was born of royal blood, and his protective father kept him oblivious when it came to the suffering world outside his home. To do this, his own father hid away people who were old, sick, and suffering from poverty. According to history, fate made a way for Siddhartha to see those who were plagued with diseases, the old, and those who were suffering. This became the reason for his depression, and the catalyst for his spiritual journey when he turned 29 years old.

Today, Buddhist meditation involves understanding his teachings: *the Noble Eightfold Path and the Four Noble Truths*. In teaching others about compassion and the truth about suffering, he was able to conquer his own depression.

Celebrities

Hollywood is not always glitz and glam. Within it, there are real human issues that many tend to overlook. After all, how can the famous and the rich be depressed? Well, you'll be surprised at how many of them are battling with this problem. The fact is: money and fame isn't everything. Depression can affect anyone regardless of their standing in life.

Lady Gaga

With her eccentric looks and powerful voice that captivates audiences worldwide, it's easy to believe that Lady Gaga has no reason to be depressed—but this is far from the truth.

DEPRESSION

In an interview with Billboard magazine, Gaga revealed that she has been plagued with anxiety and depression her entire life. This is why her mission nowadays is to help the younger generation — those who are prone to feeling disconnected to others despite staying connected through the Internet — face their emotional struggles bravely. Since then, she's become an advocate for people who are struggling with depression, abuse, and bullying.

The Rock

Even a rock is forced to face extreme weather in order to become sturdier. Dwayne "The Rock" Johnson shares this message to people who may be going through a difficult time in their lives.

He says that the important thing to remember when you are depressed is that you are not alone; that you are not the first person to be depressed, and that you are not the last to recover from it. When he was in his early twenties, he became depressed when his football career started fading. He shares that this was the lowest point in his life, and that he was literally living in his parents' basement.

He ultimately left his football dreams and tried his hand at wrestling. This was the best decision he made, and his career took off. But none of that would have happened had he not made the valiant effort to fight his depression. His story tells us to believe in ourselves and to continue pushing forward.

Cara Delevingne

Looking at Cara now, with her energetic and jolly persona sending people into fits of laughter, one would be hard-pressed to think about her being depressed. However, behind those jokes is someone who has battled hard and conquered their issues with depression.

As Delevingne started rising to stardom, her emotional state slowly began its descent. She revealed that she suffered from anxiety, depression, and self-hatred when she was just 15. Her teenage life consisted of harmful behavior, therapy sessions, and psychotropic drugs. Suicidal thoughts also began to form in her head. It was a song, she says, that really opened her eyes to the reality of her situation. One song that motivated the change in her and slowly, but surely, made her veer away from drugs and take the necessary steps towards getting better.

You can see here that even the smallest of catalysts can bring about significant changes.

Owen Wilson

Onscreen, Wilson was funny, comedic, and jolly. Behind the camera, his life was riddled with relationship problems and addiction issues. In fact, Wilson devastated friends, family, and fans when he attempted suicide. It became fodder for gossip and at that point, many believed that it was the end of his career as well. Whie still remaining quite mum about his struggles and the things he does to maintain stability, those closest to him have commented that his sons were the reason why he began to put his life back together once more.

It's all about finding a reason, isn't it? Find a purpose to keep doing what you do and fighting every single day to overcome the problem.

Demi Lovato

A few years ago, the former Disney star Demi Lovato suffered from depression which led her to undergo treatment for non-suicidal cutting, bulimia, and anorexia. Lovato was diagnosed with bipolar disorder, which led to her episodes of extreme shifts in mood, activity, and energy levels. These extreme shifts greatly affected her daily life and caused her more frustration.

Through these treatments and, of course, a firm belief in her ability to recover, we see Demi today as a confident young woman. Happy in her own body with a strong self-image, and advocating this particular cause. Giving back and supporting others in their own battles is a positive affirmation in itself — a motivation to keep going.

J.K. Rowling

Before her book started became the bestseller we know today, Rowling was a single mother who was writing in cafes while her baby was sleeping beside her. She was penniless and battling with her own issues.

In a 2012 interview, Rowling admitted that she was engulfed with depression at the time and that dark period was what inspired the series' most unnerving characters: the dementors. These were the dark-cloaked figures whose sole purpose was to "suck" out the happiness and life from any witch or wizard who might be unfortunate enough to encounter them. They represented the feelings she was struggling with at the time—a truly scary thought, if one were to think about it.

Fortunately, the author did not give into it and continued writing. She attributes her recovery to the books and that the process of writing them helped her overcome her own "dementors," much like Harry did in the books.

Ellen DeGeneres

The beloved talk show host, who revealed her sexuality in 1997, suffered a meltdown in her career after coming out. She was left unemployed as her sitcom was cancelled, and this became the ultimate reason for her depressive episodes. DeGeneres realized that there was no other reason for other people treating her the way they did other than her sexuality.

Later, she also revealed that she felt a lot of anger apart from depression, as her decision to come out publicly as gay gave others the license to start talking about her negatively, even making rude jokes about her announcement. Her role as Dory in the film *Finding Nemo* became a huge help, not only to her emotional and mental health, but also to her career.

DEPRESSION

These stories are not meant to put you down or compare your progress to theirs—not at all! As we have pointed out earlier, finding someone inspiring or simply reading the story of a person with whom you share the same issues with can actually help boost your motivation. What these stories remind us of is the fact that depression can be defeated, there is a way of overcoming it, and that the path towards recovery would be different for every individual. The bottom line is that IT CAN BE DONE!

We hope that their stories inspired you in some way and enabled you to see that you are not alone in the struggle. People from all walks of life, at any age, can suffer from depression. Nothing is wrong with you and this is not something you should be ashamed of. Instead, allow it to become your fuel to do better and become better.

CONCLUSION

Thank you for reading all the way to the end. I really hope you received value from this book and that it will allow you to cure depression naturally and permanently.

As you are already aware, in today's world, depression is a common mental condition. While a few medical procedures have proved effective at dealing with the condition, natural remedies have remained the easiest, safest, and most effective ways to deal with depression and manage it for good.

By incorporating the natural techniques highlighted in this book to help treat depression, you will overcome depression faster than you ever thought you could. Implement these strategies because they can empower you to return to a normal life that is free from worries and the threat of spiraling down.

And remember to be consistent. It will not help if you try these techniques for a week or two and then give up. Build the habit by everyday practice. Start small. Do not take on too much at the same time. It will only discourage you and you'll jump to conclusions that it does not work. It does work! It only requires time, patience and some self-discipline. After all, it took you a while to come where you are. Do not be too harsh on yourself. Take it slowly and you will beat depression once for all.

Thank you!

Now, I would like to ask for a small favor. Could you be so kind as to leave your honest review?

Each review is worth its weight in gold as it's of tremendous help to increase the book's visibility and help the author reach more readers. Reaching 50, and then 100 reviews, is a vitally important milestone for every author.

If you're strapped for time, even just one or two sentences will do.

Thank you so much,
Sarah

MORE BOOKS BY SARAH

Mindfulness. Simple Techniques You Need to Know to Live in The Moment and Relieve Stress, Anxiety and Depression for Good (Mindfulness Book Series, Book 1)

Mindful Eating. How to Stop Binge Eating and Overeating, Lose Weight Permanently and Forever Heal Your Relationship with Food (Mindfulness Book Series, Book 3)

Mindfulness for Social Anxiety Relief. Learn How to Regain Control of Your Life and Overcome Social Anxiety, Fear, Worry and Self-Criticism Forever (Mindfulness Book Series, Book 2)

Leaky Gut No More. 12 Proven Ways to Heal Leaky Gut Naturally. Boost Metabolism and Lose Weight Permanently – Look and Feel Great. (The Gut Repair Book Series, Book1)

GAPS Diet. 30 Nutrient-Dense Recipes to Alleviate Chronic Inflammation, Repair the Gut Wall and Regain Energy (The Gut Repair Book Series, Book2)

✓ ***Fermented Vegetables***: Top 30 Delicious Recipes for Fermented Vegetables and Probiotic Foods that will Restore your Optimal Gut Health (The Gut Repair Book Series, Book3)

Habits: *The Most Effective Habits to Overcome Life's Biggest Challenges and Achieve Your Most Important Goals*

Printed in Poland
by Amazon Fulfillment
Poland Sp. z o.o., Wrocław